AMERICA'S SHARK LADY

The Complete Adventures of Eugenie Clark

by
Ann McGovern

SCHOLASTIC INC.
New York Toronto London Auckland Sydney
Mexico City New Delhi Hong Kong Buenos Aires

Photograph credits: p. 68, Niki Konstantinou; p. 81, 112, Stan Waterman; p. 84, David Doubilet; p. 91, Emory Kristoff/National Geographic Image Collection; p. 105, Chuck Davis/IMAX Film Production.

Page from Eugenie Clark's notebooks, p.97, courtesy of Eugenie Clark. Dr. Clark also provided photographs on the following pages: 6, 13, 17, 20, 23, 24, 32, 35, 44, 51, 59, 95.

ISBN 0-439-63188-2

12 11 10 9 8 7 6 5 4 3 2 1   4 5 6 7 8 9/0

Printed in the U.S.A.   40

First bind-up edition, March 2004

For Eugenie Clark's grandson, Eli
For my grandchildren, Sharon, Chris, and Dennis

AMERICA'S SHARK LADY

The Complete Adventures of Eugenie Clark

Book One
"Someday I Will Swim with the Sharks"

Book Two
More Adventures of the Shark Lady

Contents

Book Two: More Adventures of the Shark Lady

For a list of the awards and honors Eugenie Clark has received, visit her Web site at www.sharklady.com.

BOOK ONE

"Someday I Will Swim with the Sharks"

1
A Very Special Saturday

"**W**ake up, Genie," Mama called. "We have to go downtown soon."

Eugenie Clark mumbled into her pillow. Who wants to go downtown on a Saturday? Saturdays were for climbing rocks and trees with Norma, her best friend. Saturdays were for digging up fat worms, bringing home bugs and snakes — making sure that Grandma didn't see them.

Those were the good Saturdays. But today was different. Her friend Norma had to go shopping with her mother. Grandma wasn't feeling well and needed peace and quiet.

There was no place for nine-year-old Eugenie to be except with Mama at work.

Mama worked in a big building in downtown New York City. She sold newspapers at the newsstand in the lobby.

As the rumbling subway train sped downtown, Mama looked at her daughter's sad face and wished there was something she could do to make Eugenie happier. Eugenie's father had died in 1924 when she was a baby, so Mama had to work extra hard to earn enough money to take care of the family. Working extra hard meant working Saturday mornings, too.

The subway train pulled into their station and they got out. A sign at the top of the subway stairs said: TO THE AQUARIUM.

"That's a good idea," Mama said. "I'll leave you at the Aquarium and I'll pick you up at lunchtime. That will be more fun for you than sitting around the newsstand all morning."

Eugenie walked through the doors of the Aquarium and into the world of fish.

She walked among the tanks filled with strange fish. Then she came to a big, mysterious-looking tank at the back. She stared at it for a long, long time. The green misty water seemed to go on and on. She leaned over the rail, her face close to the glass, and pretended that she was walking on the bottom of the sea.

Eugenie went to the Aquarium the next Saturday. And the next Saturday. And the Saturday after that. She went to the Aquarium on all the cold Saturdays, the rainy and snowy Saturdays of autumn and winter. Sometimes her best friend, Norma, came with her. But often she was alone with the fish.

Eugenie read about fish, too. She read about a scientist who put a diving helmet on his head and went deep under the waves. He walked on the bottom of the sea with the fish swimming around him.

"Someday I'll walk with the fish, too," she said.

Mama had taught Eugenie to swim before she was two years old.

In the summertime, Mama took her to the beach. When Mama came out of the water, her long jet-black hair streamed down her back.

Nine-year-old Eugenie with her mother.

Eugenie thought she looked like pictures she had seen of beautiful pearl divers of the Orient. Mama was Japanese.

Mama was a good swimmer, and in the summertime Eugenie loved to watch her swim with long, graceful strokes.

Now, in the autumn and in the winter, Eugenie watched the very best swimmers — the fish in the Aquarium. She found all the fish fascinating — the smallest fish glowing like tiny jewels and the fish with fluttering fins that looked like fairy wings. But it was the biggest streamlined fish in the Aquarium that she came back to again and again.

She watched the big shark swimming, turning, swimming, turning, never resting its long, graceful body. She watched it and lost track of time.

Mysterious shark, she thought. *Someday I'll swim with sharks, too.*

2
Three Fish, Four Fish —
More and More Fish

"**G**ood morning, Genie. Great weather for fish," the guard at the Aquarium said one rainy Saturday.

Eugenie laughed. "Hi, Mr. Walker. Are my friends here yet?"

Mr. Walker nodded. "Oh, yes," he said. "They always show up on rainy days." He watched the skinny dark-haired girl go through the door.

Friends, ha! he thought. *Those good-for-nothing bums that come here to get out of the rain.* Mr. Walker shook his head. *Never saw anything like it. A bunch of bums paying attention to a little girl talking about fish.*

Inside the Aquarium, Eugenie moved from one fish tank to another. A small group of men in dirty, worn-out clothes followed her.

"Hey, teacher!" one man said. "This fish has whiskers, just like mine."

"Like the whiskers on a cat, too," Eugenie said. "Maybe that's why it's called a catfish. See? Watch how it uses its whiskers to find food on the bottom of the tank."

The men always called her teacher, half in fun. One of her secret dreams was to be a teacher like wonderful Miss Reilly, her favorite teacher in all the world.

Miss Reilly took Eugenie's fourth-grade class on field trips to the woods to gather moss, ferns, and salamanders. Eugenie hoped that they could come to the Aquarium, too. Miss Reilly said she would like the class to see "Genie's fish."

Genie's fish. Genie's fish. An idea began to grow.

The next Saturday at lunchtime, the idea spilled out. Every Saturday, Eugenie and Mama ate lunch at a tiny Japanese restaurant owned by their good friend, Nobusan. Today, Eugenie's mind was whirling with her new idea.

"Just think," she said. "Some people have beautiful fish in their own home and watch them all the time. Mama, Christmas is coming soon." Eugenie crossed her fingers and made a wish.

After lunch, Eugenie and Mama went to a pet shop to pick out the Christmas present. They chose a large aquarium with gravel and stones. They bought plants to make it look natural. They bought some snails to keep it clean.

Then came the best part — picking out the fish. They chose guppies and angelfish, green swordtails and black-speckled redfish.

"Stop!" Eugenie's mother laughed. "I've spent more than I planned for Christmas." Just then Eugenie saw a red-banded clownfish. "Oh, Mama, could I have just one more," she begged, "for my birthday?"

"But your birthday isn't until May," Mama said. The clownfish swam to the front of the tank.

"It is pretty," Mama said. "All right, we'll buy it."

Before they left the shop that day, they lost track of how many years' worth of Christmas and birthday presents Eugenie had used up.

Before long, the small apartment was crowded with fish of all kinds. Mama became fascinated with fish, too. Sometimes she would bring home little white boxes with fish swimming inside. When that happened, Eugenie knew that Mama had spent her lunch hour and maybe her lunch money in the pet shop.

Eugenie joined the Queens County Aquarium Society and became its youngest member. She learned how to keep good records of her pets. She wrote down their scientific names, the dates she got each fish, and what happened to them.

When some of Eugenie's fish had babies, hundreds of tiny wriggling fish filled the aquarium. Once Eugenie thought of going into the fish business selling baby fish.

But Grandma said NO!

3
Trouble with Grandma

Eugenie's zoo grew. Besides hundreds of fish, there were salamanders, toads, and snakes.

When Eugenie went to college, she was more interested in fish than in any other animal. But in order to learn about fish, she had to study all kinds of creatures.

She learned how to cut up — dissect — dead animals, which is the best way to find out about their different parts.

Once, a friendly pet-shop owner gave Eugenie a monkey that had died. She took it home and put it in the refrigerator so it wouldn't spoil and smell bad. That evening, Grandma opened the refrigerator door and saw the dead monkey on the shelf. She screamed and ran out of the kitchen. "No more dead animals in this house!" she said.

"Why doesn't Genie study typing?" she complained to Mama. Mama worried, too.

"Genie dear," she said, "I know you want to study and work with fish — to be an ichthyologist. But what if you can't be an ichthyologist

Eugenie was in college when this photo was taken.

right away? If you learn typing, you might be able to get a job as the secretary of a famous ichthyologist."

But Eugenie knew what she wanted to be. And so she went right on studying hard and learning about fish and other animals.

Eugenie had learned how to skin a dead animal in the lab in college, but she felt she needed more practice. One day the neighborhood grocer killed a big rat in his store and Eugenie begged to have it.

The grocer wrapped it up and she took it home. Good. There was nobody in the house. Quickly Engenie skinned it. Then she got out one of her grandmother's cooking pots.

She wanted the skeleton. She would have to boil the rat. Every five minutes Eugenie ran into the street to see if Grandma was coming. Then she ran back inside to check the pot. The rat was still boiling when Eugenie suddenly heard Grandma's footsteps outside.

What could Eugenie do?

It was too late to do anything. Grandma was standing in the kitchen doorway.

"Genie, darling," she said. "What are you cooking?"

Before Eugenie could stop her, she lifted the pot cover, peered inside, and saw the big rat's two sharp teeth. Eugenie was not allowed to cook in the kitchen again for a long time.

4
Danger in the Deep

Eugenie graduated from Hunter College in New York City in 1942. She went to California to go on with her fish studies and to work as a part-time research assistant to Dr. Carl Hubbs, a famous ichthyologist.

In those days, people who wanted to explore the bottom of the sea had to wear heavy helmets with air lines that connected them to the boat above.

Now, for the first time, Eugenie was going to walk on the sea bottom in a diving helmet!

Before Eugenie could go in the water, she had to have lessons. She had to learn how to

Dr. Carl Hubbs shows off two octopuses.

turn the air valve on the helmet to control the amount of air she breathed.

She had to know about the signals that the divers used to send messages to the boat. One tug on the signal line meant: "I'm okay." Two tugs meant "Give me more line." Three tugs meant "Take up the loose line," and four tugs meant "Danger. Pull me up." And most important, she had to stay calm in an emergency.

At last she was ready. She climbed down the boat's ladder until she was up to her neck in water. Then the heavy helmet was put on her head.

She slid down the rope until her feet touched sand. She was really on the bottom of the sea! Silvery fish swam by, so close! One fish swam right up to her helmet and looked in at her face.

Once, the sand moved under her feet and a flounder darted away. Everything seemed magical — even a clump of rocks. Coming closer she could see that the rocks had holes like windows, with lovely fish darting in and out. Colorful sponges grew over the rocks. *Like Hansel and Gretel's gingerbread house in a water forest,* she thought. *I wonder what witch of the sea lives here.*

She remembered the first time she went to the Aquarium, when she had pretended to be walking on the bottom of the sea.

Now I'm not pretending. I am really, really walking on the bottom of the sea.

She wandered along the sea bottom as if in a dream. She tried to catch some of the bold fish with her hands.

Suddenly she noticed that it was getting

harder to breathe. She turned the air valve on her helmet, but it didn't help. Soon she was gasping for air. She opened the valve more and more until it no longer turned.

Her head felt groggy. Her eyes burned. Something was terribly wrong. She started toward the boat as fast as she could. But her steps were so slow. The helmet was so heavy. Now her breath was coming in short gasps.

At last she saw the bottom of the boat. Now she could see the line hanging under the boat. With her last bit of strength, she tugged hard. Four tugs meant "Danger. Pull me up!" But she could tug on the line only once before she felt herself falling. As she fell to her knees, she thought, *No! One tug means okay. I'm not okay . . . not okay.*

Now water was beginning to seep into her helmet — cold water that brought her to her senses. As fast as she could, she got the heavy helmet off her head and let herself float up, up, up to the surface.

The men on the boat dived over the side. Strong hands reached out to her.

Safe on board she was wrapped in warm blankets and given hot coffee.

"What happened?" Dr. Hubbs asked.

Eugenie told him about her breathing trouble. "I kept opening the valve more and more, but no more air came in," she said.

A sailor on the boat laughed. "I bet you screwed the valve the wrong way and cut off your own air," he said. "Just like a girl."

Dr. Hubbs checked the diving helmet. "Wait

Eugenie had her first diving adventure from the boat named the E. W. Scripps.

a minute, sailor," he said. "Who was responsible for checking the air line? There's a leak in it. That means she was losing most of the air before it could even get into her helmet."

The sailor's face turned red. "Sorry," he mumbled.

"What a terrible thing to happen on your first dive," Dr. Hubbs said to Eugenie. "There's only one thing to do."

And that one thing was to go down to the bottom of the sea again. So as soon as the helmet was fixed, down, down, she went. And this time — as in all the helmet dives to follow — nothing went wrong.

5
Adventures in the South Seas

After studying and working with Dr. Hubbs in California for almost a year, Eugenie went back to New York. She worked at the American Museum of Natural History and studied at New York University.

Now, three years later, she was saying good-bye to Mama and her stepfather, Nobusan. Mama had married Nobusan, whom Eugenie had loved ever since she was a child.

Eugenie was flying far away to the South Sea islands. The U.S. Navy and scientists in Washington, D.C., wanted to learn more about the fish of these Pacific islands. Which ones

Eugenie at work in the lab of the American Museum of Natural History.

were safe to eat? Which ones were poisonous? Would Eugenie Clark be willing to fly nine thousand miles to collect fish and study them? Would she?! She could hardly wait.

The next few months were filled with adventure. She traveled from island to island collecting fish in the beautiful blue-green waters around the coral reefs. She wore a glass face mask so she could keep her eyes open and see clearly underwater. With her snorkel she could float on the top of the water for a long time and look down through her mask at the wonders of the Pacific reefs below.

She went diving with the native fishermen of the islands. They shared their lunches of raw fish with her and the cool white milk of coconuts.

Eugenie made friends on every island.

On the tiny island of Mog Mog, Eugenie was

The chiefs of a South Sea island welcome Eugenie to their village.

taken to meet King Ueg. He was the first king she had ever met. What would he think of her in her bare feet, her hair in pigtails, and wearing only her bathing suit? But the king didn't mind. He wasn't wearing anything but a loincloth!

On another island, she made friends with the governor and his family. The whole family helped her collect fish on the reef. The collecting trips became picnics. At night they all pitched in to sort out the fish and take notes.

Eugenie learned many things about the poisonous fish of the South Seas. She learned that some kinds of fish might be poisonous on one island but not on another. She learned that some kinds were dangerous to eat at certain times of the year but perfectly safe at other times.

Eugenie never knew what adventures she would face each day. One afternoon, she was in the water collecting fish. She had been swimming a long time and she was tired. She was far out on the reef where the water was very deep.

Suddenly she sensed something behind her. She turned. A big shark was swimming toward her!

She stopped swimming. The shark was coming closer and closer. Eugenie knew she should be frightened. Her mind told her to be frightened. But she wasn't. All she could do was admire the shark. It was so streamlined, so graceful. The shark came so close to her that she could almost have reached out and touched it. Then it turned and swam off, down into the deep.

Suddenly Eugenie remembered the promise she had made to herself long ago. "Someday I'll swim with sharks," she had said when she was a little girl at the Aquarium in New York City.

Now that dream, too, had come true.

6
Fishing for Sharks

Eugenie was back in New York City. Snow was falling softly outside her window. She was thinking of warmer days in warm waters.

So much had happened since she had seen her first shark in the waters of the South Sea Islands. Eugenie had gone on with her studies in ichthyology and had earned high honors. Now she was called Dr. Eugenie Clark! She had won scholarships to study fish in many parts of the world. And she had married a medical doctor named Ilias Konstantinou. Best of all, they had Hera, a darling baby girl. Somehow Dr. Eugenie Clark had also found time to write a book about her adventures called *Lady With a Spear*.

In her book, she had written about a marine laboratory on the Red Sea where she had studied and worked for a year. Thousands of people read her book. Anne and William Vanderbilt of Florida read it, too.

There was no marine laboratory in the western part of Florida where the Vanderbilts lived. They called Eugenie and invited her to meet with them.

"It would be great if we had a marine lab here," Mr. Vanderbilt said to her. "Something like the one you described in your book. What do you think? Would you consider starting one and being the director?"

Her own lab! It was a thrilling thought.

"Make it a place where people can learn more about the sea," Mr. Vanderbilt said. The Vanderbilts were very rich. They used some of their money for worthwhile projects, like the Marine Laboratory.

Eugenie's husband liked the idea of being a doctor in Florida. The warm Florida sunshine would be wonderful for little Hera and for the new baby who would soon be born. Even Mama and Nobusan were excited. "Maybe we'll move down and open a restaurant," Mama said. "There isn't one Japanese restaurant in the state of Florida."

Six months later, in early January 1955, Dr. Eugenie Clark opened the doors of a small wooden building. A sign over the door read CAPE HAZE MARINE LABORATORY. Nearby were beaches, bays, islands, and the Gulf of Mexico. The sea was right outside the door!

Eugenie couldn't wait to see what treasures were in those waters. That very afternoon she and a local fisherman, Beryl Chadwick, netted many fish, including sea horses. Eugenie was eager to start the job of identifying all the local fishes. Beryl would be her assistant.

The very next day, Eugenie got a phone call from a Dr. John Heller. He needed shark livers for his important medical research. He had heard about the new lab. Could Eugenie possibly get him a shark?

Eugenie turned to her fisherman assistant.

"Beryl," she said. "Do you know how to catch a shark?"

He gave her a funny look. Eugenie soon found out that Beryl could catch almost anything in the sea that moved. He got to work right away making a shark fishing line.

Dr. Heller and his wife came to the lab to help catch the shark.

Soon Beryl had the line ready. Steel chains made it strong. Big steel hooks on the line were baited with fish. Beryl set the line two miles out from the shore.

First thing the next morning, Eugenie, Beryl, and Dr. and Mrs. Heller went out in the lab's boat to check the line.

The first hook was empty.

The second hook was empty.

So was the third.

"Look at this!" Beryl shouted. A steel chain was twisted. The thick metal hook was bent out of shape.

Beryl kept on pulling in the line and putting new bait on the empty hooks. Suddenly the line became hard to pull. Dr. Heller grabbed the line to help.

Then Eugenie saw it — a large gray shark streaking through the water!

The shark was hooked but it was still alive. They saw its staring eyes. As its jaws moved they saw its sharp triangular teeth.

Eugenie could hardly believe their luck.

"What did you expect on a shark line?" Beryl beamed. "Goldfish?"

Before the day was over, they had caught another shark. Together the two big sharks weighed more than seven hundred pounds. It took six men to drag them up to shore. Now Dr. Heller had the shark livers he needed.

By the end of that first week, they had caught twelve more, mostly dusky and sand-bar sharks.

Eugenie wanted to study sharks in captivity. The lab needed a place to keep sharks alive. So next to the lab's dock, a big pen was built for holding sharks and other large fish.

Eugenie looked down into the waters of the

shark pen where the big fish were swimming. *There is so much to learn about these fascinating fish,* she thought. She could hardly wait to get started.

Dr. Heller removes a shark liver as Eugenie and an assistant take notes.

7
Children Everywhere

The lab continued to grow.

From the beginning, scientists came to the lab to work on their research projects.

There was a library just for books and magazines about sea life. There were thirty tanks for fish and other sea creatures. New shark pens were built.

Every day people brought in buckets filled with some swimming or creeping creatures of the sea. They brought in snakes and turtles. One man came in with an alligator almost as big as Eugenie. Beryl made a pond for it under the shade of a palm tree.

During the twelve exciting years she worked at the lab, Eugenie had more children. Now Hera and her little sister, Aya, had two brothers, Tak and Niki.

Eugenie's children were never afraid of the water. Before they were a week old, Eugenie had taught them to love the water. All of them could swim long before they could walk.

Mama and Nobusan came to Florida and opened a Japanese restaurant near Eugenie and her family. When the children were little, Eugenie's mother often looked after them.

As they grew older, Eugenie's children spent more time at the lab. There were always lots of children around. Visiting scientists often brought their children with them. Neighborhood children liked to help at the lab. The children helped haul up sharks to be weighed. They helped pull in netfuls of fish to the beach.

Some days it seemed that there were children everywhere — children peering into microscopes, children fishing from the docks, children looking at the books in the library.

Eugenie measures a tiger shark at Cape Haze.

Teachers brought their classes to visit. Eugenie talked to the schoolchildren about fish. Beryl showed them the alligator, the snakes, the turtles, and the big shark pen.

One day Beryl took a class out to the shark pen to show them Rosy, his favorite shark. The big nurse shark was at the bottom of the pen, out of sight. Beryl splashed his hand in the water to call her. He turned his head away for a moment to say something to the children. At that instant, Rosy swam up from below, lifted her head out of the water, and touched Beryl's hand, ever so gently. One of the children thought it looked as if Rosy were kissing Beryl's hand. But ever since that day, one of Beryl's fingers has been a little bit shorter.

That was the only time anyone was ever hurt by a shark at the lab.

As more and more scientists came to study, the lab got more and more equipment.

For Eugenie, the scuba-diving equipment was the most exciting. No longer did she have to hold her breath to stay underwater or wear a heavy helmet attached by an air hose to a boat. Now with a scuba tank of air on her back, she could stay in the underwater world for almost an hour to study the habits of the fish on a reef. And she could go deeper — deep down to one hundred feet or more, where the biggest fish — the sharks — swim.

"I was doing what I always wanted to do most," she wrote later, "studying sharks and other fish, with everything in one place: collecting grounds, the lab, and my home and family."

But there were problems, too.

One Sunday afternoon, Eugenie was working at the lab. She looked out of the window and gasped. A little boy about four years old was sitting on the wooden feeding platform of the shark pen! And he was dangling his feet in the water! Eugenie dashed out of the lab and pulled the child to safety.

His parents were wandering around outside. They had paid no attention to the signs marked DANGER — SHARKS.

"We didn't see any sharks in the pen," they told Eugenie, "so we thought it was empty."

"There's a big shark swimming there right now," Eugenie said. "You're lucky it ate all it wanted yesterday or your boy's dangling foot might have been part of its dinner today!"

Another morning when she came to work, Eugenie found a tiger shark dead in the shark pen. A round hoop had been jammed over its head. Someone had climbed over the fence and killed it.

New signs marked KEEP OUT were posted all over and a new fence was put up.

Everyone has a lot to say about sharks attacking people, Eugenie thought sadly. *But what about people who attack sharks?*

8
Who Said Sharks Are Stupid?

Eugenie kept on learning new things from the sharks they caught on the shark lines. They caught hammerheads, black-fin sharks, small dogfish sharks, lemon sharks, nurse sharks, bull sharks, and tiger sharks. Once in a while they caught a great white shark.

Eugenie's success in keeping sharks in captivity became known far and wide. Scientists from all over the world were coming to the lab to study sharks.

They cut open the stomachs to find out what sharks ate. They learned that sharks ate more than forty kinds of fish, including eels, stingrays, and other sharks. They found that sharks also ate octopus, crab, and shrimp. Sometimes they ate a sea turtle or a sea bird or, once in a great while, a porpoise.

Eugenie found that the most interesting part of her work was studying live sharks. She got to know the sharks so well that she could tell one shark from another by its behavior.

Eugenie wanted to learn more about their feeding habits. *How much food does it take to keep a nine-foot lemon shark alive?* Eugenie wondered. She learned that it took only two pounds of food a day to keep it healthy and active.

One day, a Dr. Lester Aronson came to the lab. His work was the study of animal behavior.

"Has anyone ever made a study of the learning behavior of sharks?" Eugenie asked him.

He told her no. He said that everyone thought sharks were rather stupid.

"But you certainly have a good setup here for testing to see if they could learn a simple task," he told her. That was all she needed to hear. Before the day was over, they had worked out a plan.

First, they designed the equipment to train the sharks. They made a wooden square and painted it white.

Eugenie placed the wooden square, called the target, into the shark pen. A shark had to learn that if it pressed its nose against the target, it would get food as a reward.

In a couple of months, Eugenie's sharks learned to press the target every time they wanted food.

Then she made the test harder. First a shark had to press the target as usual. Then it had to turn and swim to the other end of the shark pen to get its reward.

Eugenie's plan worked! She proved that sharks could indeed learn a simple task.

One December day, Eugenie learned something else about sharks. She set up her experiment as usual. But the sharks didn't press the target. Had they forgotten everything she had taught them? It turned out that sharks lost interest in food when the water got colder.

In February, when the water in the shark pen warmed up again, the sharks began once more to press the target for food, as if they had never lost a day of practice.

Now Eugenie knew that sharks were indeed smart enough to learn. And that they had a good memory as well!

9
A Visit to the Palace

One summer, Dr. Aronson's sixteen-year-old son, Freddie, came to work at the lab. He was especially interested in setting up experiments that would help people learn how sharks use their eyes. Could sharks tell light from dark? Could they tell the difference between horizontal stripes ≡ and vertical stripes |||?

Freddie worked with Eugenie Clark for three summers. With the help of two other high-school students, Freddie designed new equipment with several targets to test the sharks.

He trained a little two-foot nurse shark to

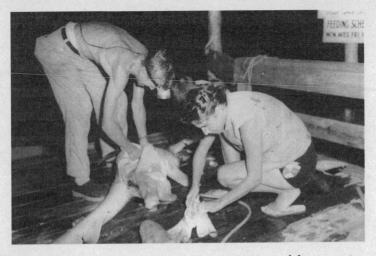

On a dock at Cape Haze, Eugenie and her assistant examine nurse sharks.

swim to a target that was lit and press it when it wanted food. The shark learned in five days — a new record.

In the fall of 1965, just as Freddie was about to return to school in New York, Eugenie received an invitation to come to Japan. Her book, *Lady With a Spear,* had been published there. It was one of the most popular books in the country. She was asked to appear on TV shows. Japanese scientists wanted her to visit their labs. And best of all, the crown prince wanted to meet her! Like his father, the emperor, Crown Prince Akihito was interested in fish and marine biology.

"What do you do when you are invited to the palace of the crown prince?" Eugenie wanted to know.

"You take him a present," her friends said.

"But what do you give a prince?" She turned to Freddie. "How about your trained shark?" she said as a joke. "I'm sure the prince doesn't have one!"

Freddie thought it was a wonderful idea. So did everyone else.

"I'll make you a special box for the shark," Freddie said. "Everything will be easy to carry."

He stayed up all that night. By morning the box was finished. It was just the right size for a two-foot shark. It was as big as a large hat box. The box was lined with plastic and filled with enough water to cover the little shark.

Eugenie was worried. "Suppose the shark dies on the way? Suppose I walk into the palace and say to the prince, 'Here's a trained shark for you!' And suppose the shark doesn't perform?"

By now Eugenie was so worried that she was almost sorry she had accepted the royal invitation. But everyone else was excited about a shark traveling to Japan as a present for a prince.

The airline sent men to help with the shark. The shark had a seat on the plane next to Eugenie at no extra cost. When the plane stopped in Hawaii, the director of the aquarium there even arranged for the shark to have a swim in one of his tanks!

As the plane approached the airport in Tokyo, Eugenie took a last peek at the shark. The shark seemed fine, but Eugenie's heart was fluttering like a butterfly. She closed the cover, and with trembling hands she carried the shark off the plane.

A huge welcoming party was waiting for her. There were scientists and professors, newspaper reporters and TV cameras. A giant truck carrying a huge saltwater aquarium stood by. The little shark that had traveled halfway around the world in a box looked even smaller swimming around in an aquarium built for a twelve-foot shark!

Eugenie was still nervous as she was led to the palace. With many bows and with great ceremony, she was presented to the crown prince.

The crown prince made Eugenie feel comfortable right away. He asked her many questions about her work and Eugenie forgot to be scared.

The prince was eager to see the shark perform. It had been put into a low tank set on top of a table in the middle of the room. Now the prince could get a really good look at the shark.

Curtains were drawn to darken the room so that everyone could see the lighted target. One of the palace servants stood by with a platter of reward food for the shark. Eugenie thought it looked like food fit for the prince himself. Slices of lobster were beautifully arranged in the shape of a flower.

Everyone was ready. Eugenie's heart was

beating fast. Would the shark be able to perform?

The shark swam around the tank. Then it headed straight for the right target — to the one that was lit up.

Eugenie gave a sigh of relief. The prince and his court clapped their hands. With jeweled chopsticks, the servant placed a slice of the lobster flower before the shark.

After that, the prince showed Eugenie the palace aquarium. A special aquarium had been prepared for Eugenie's shark.

Then it was tea time. Together they sipped tea and ate cookies and talked about fish. Eugenie was surprised to learn that the prince had never learned to dive, had never even looked at fish through a glass face mask.

Two years after her visit to Japan, she got a telegram. The crown prince was passing through the United States on his way home from South America. He wanted to stop in Florida and see her.

Eugenie thought the crown prince would be

tired after his long trip. But they talked and talked about fish for hours. The other men in the room were half-asleep.

At midnight, the prince asked her, "Dr. Clark would you do me a favor? Could you teach me to dive?"

"When do you want to learn?" she asked him.

"How about five o'clock this morning?" he said.

And so a few hours later, just as the sun was coming up, Eugenie taught the crown prince many things, like how to spit in his mask to keep the glass from fogging and how to empty the mask if it filled up with sea water.

There was only a short time left for a swim in deeper waters.

On the beach, the prince's royal guards in rolled-up pants watched with worried faces as the American "Shark Lady" and Japan's crown prince disappeared beneath the waves.

10
Into the Caves of the Sleeping Sharks

Soon the happy days at the lab were over for Eugenie. Her mother had died. Eugenie's marriage had come to an end and she decided to move north with her children. Her stepfather, Nobusan, followed soon after.

Eugenie knew she was leaving the lab in good hands. Dr. Perry Gilbert, who conducted important studies on sharks, became the new director.

The next years were busy for Eugenie. She wrote a book about her exciting years at the lab, called *The Lady and the Sharks*.

Eugenie Clark's long-ago dream of becoming a teacher came true. She became Professor of Zoology at the University of Maryland in 1973. She shared her great knowledge and her love of fish with her students. Her students brought their friends to hear Professor Clark talk about her underwater adventures in far-away places. "Study what fascinates you the most," she told her students.

As for herself, she never stopped studying and learning. There was always an important project to work on, something new to discover, or some underwater mystery to solve.

Eugenie isn't afraid to get close to a reef shark.

For instance, there was the mystery of the "sleeping" sharks.

Eugenie had her first clue from an old friend, Ramón Bravo, an underwater naturalist and photographer from Mexico. He sent word that big sharks had been discovered in an underwater cave, sixty-seven feet below the sea. These sharks seemed to be sleeping!

"They are not the slow-moving nurse sharks often found in caves," he told her, "but streamlined 'man-eating' requiem sharks."

Would she come and see for herself?

If it were really true, it certainly would be amazing, Eugenie thought. Everyone, including scientists, thought these sharks had to keep moving to keep water flowing over their gills. Water contains oxygen that all sharks need to stay alive.

Eugenie could take only a few days away from her teaching to go to Mexico. When she got there she dived to the underwater cave. She saw many beautiful fish in the cave but there were no sharks. Then, just as she was coming out, a shark slipped into the cave.

"I don't know how I can prove to you that these sharks do sleep in these caves," Ramón said. "Maybe I have to put them in pajamas and give them an alarm clock." He begged her to return as soon as she could.

The next year she was back with a research team made up of several of her students, Mexican divers, underwater photographers, and her nineteen-year-old daughter, Aya.

This time she saw the sharks in the caves.

"It was really unbelievable," Eugenie wrote in *National Geographic* magazine. "There I was, face to face with one of the sea's most deadly denizens, in the most dangerous situation possible — the shark, crowded, backed into a corner — and I'd never been more thrilled. It was an unforgettable moment in my life."

There was so much Eugenie wanted to learn. The Mexican divers told her that these sharks could be touched, even lifted gently, without becoming dangerous. Sometimes when they were poked, the sharks would swim away. Sometimes, they settled back to their sleeplike state again.

Why? Why do big, streamlined sharks stop swimming and go into this sleeplike state? From her studies, Eugenie knew that it took more energy for a streamlined shark to stop swimming than to keep on swimming. When a shark is at rest, it has to work harder to keep the water flowing through its gills.

Eugenie and her assistants searched for answers in the caves.

They noticed that the sharks in the caves were very clean. Their skins were free of parasites — tiny animals that grow on the skins of big fish.

One day, Eugenie saw a little remora fish cleaning a shark in a cave. The remora was swimming in and out of each gill removing parasites. Then it nibbled at parasites all over the shark's head and down the shark's big body!

Could these caves be cleaning stations for sharks? It certainly looked like it.

There was so much to learn and so little time left. In a few days, she had to be back at the university.

Anita George, one of Eugenie's graduate students, wanted to get some last-minute information on the sleeping sharks in the cave. Two divers went down with her to the underwater cave. Anita took notes on her special underwater clipboard.

One of the divers flashed a bright light to take a picture with his underwater camera. Perhaps it was the light that did it. The shark woke up! It swept toward the opening of the cave, smashing its tail into Anita. It almost knocked off her face mask.

The shark was coming right toward her! She had only one thing with which to defend herself — her clipboard. And she used it to push the big shark aside!

That night nobody got much sleep.

Time was up. There were no more days left for new adventures or to find answers to questions. The puzzle of the sleeping sharks was still a mystery.

11
The Puzzle of the Sleeping Sharks

The next summer, Eugenie and her assistants came back to the sleeping shark caves of Mexico.

Would they find the answers to the mystery of the sleeping sharks this time? Their tests had shown that the water in the caves was, at times, different from the water in the open sea. There was more oxygen, for one thing. And fresh water was seeping up into the caves from streams under the ocean floor.

Perhaps something in the water is making the sharks groggy, Eugenie thought.

"Perhaps our sleeping sharks are drawn

into the caves first to get cleaned, and second to enjoy the pleasant sensations," Dr. Clark wrote.

And did the sharks really sleep in the caves? The more Eugenie studied them, the more she thought they didn't. When Eugenie and her assistant were in the caves, the sharks' eyes followed their every move.

Eugenie wanted to find out more about the sharks' sleeplike state. *Do fish sleep the way we sleep*, she wondered, *the way other animals sleep?*

"It's very difficult to run tests on fish," Eugenie said to her assistant. "We're still working on ways it can be done with sharks in captivity and with sharks in the open sea."

Eugenie wrote in her *National Geographic* article: "Perhaps in deeper waters, in other parts of the world, requiem sharks also sleep."

She was right. In 1976, Eugenie was invited to Japan again. Her graduate student, Anita George, came too, and this time Eugenie took along her stepfather, Nobusan. He was more than 70 years old and was a wonderful help.

He spoke Japanese and he also learned to keep charts of the breathing rates of sharks.

Eugenie and her assistants dived in many places. In one bay, Eugenie and Anita saw more than a hundred sharks — more than they had ever seen before at one time! Some were swimming around in the shallow end of the bay. Eugenie and Anita stood in the water taking notes while sharks swam around them.

Some of the sharks were in underwater caves, piled on top of each other, and they seemed to be asleep!

Eugenie found two different kinds of "sleeping" sharks in Japan. One of them was the streamlined requiem shark she had studied in Mexico. The other was the white-tip reef shark, a sluggish shark that spends a good deal of time on the bottom of the reef. What made these sharks go into a sleeplike state like the fast-moving requiem sharks did? More tests had to be made, more sharks studied.

Once, a scientist took her to see thirty sharks in another underwater cave not far from Tokyo. Eugenie swam around, petting them, and they didn't wake up. The scientist made her promise she would never tell where the cave was.

"If people in Tokyo knew about this place," he said, "they would all race down here to hunt the sharks for food."

"And people say sharks are killers," Eugenie said. "Isn't it odd that people kill and eat more sharks than sharks eat people!"

At the end of the summer, Eugenie returned to her classes at the university.

"Where will you go next to solve the mystery of the sleeping sharks?" her students asked her.

Dr. Clark, a popular teacher at the University of Maryland, poses in her office.

"I hear that in the Red Sea there is a cave." Eugenie's eyes sparkled. "And in that cave there are five sleeping sharks. They are the white-tip reef shark, the same kind of shark I saw in Japan. This summer I'll go back to the Red Sea.

"It's like a puzzle," Eugenie told her students. "You think you have the pieces put together and then, suddenly, one piece doesn't fit, and you're off on something else."

12
A Mighty Shark
and a Little Fish

Several years earlier, Engenie had gone to Israel to do research at the Marine Laboratory on the Red Sea. She was studying a little fish they called the Moses sole.

The first time she caught the Moses sole in her net, she was surprised to see a bit of white milky fluid oozing out along its fins. She reached out and touched the fins. The milky stuff felt slippery and slimy. Her fingers felt tight and tingly. That milky fluid might be poisonous!

Eugenie ran tests in the lab, and then she began experiments in the sea. She put the

Moses sole in a large plastic bag that fit over a branch of coral where many little fish lived. Next she squeezed the Moses sole through the plastic bag. She squeezed until a few drops of milk came out. In minutes, every small fish that had been swimming in the bag was dead, killed by the poison of the Moses sole.

What would happen to bigger, more dangerous fish? she wondered. She began testing the Moses sole with sharks in the lab. She tied the little fish to a line in the shark tank. First the sharks swam toward the Moses sole with their mouths open, ready to gobble the little fish. Then, with their jaws still wide open, the sharks jerked away. They thrashed and leaped about the tank, shaking their heads wildly from side to side. All the while, the Moses sole kept swimming, as if nothing unusual was happening.

Next, Eugenie put ordinary fish right next to the Moses sole on the line. The sharks kept away from those fish, too.

For the next test, Eugenie washed the skin of a Moses sole with alcohol. She dropped the fish into the shark tank. The little fish was inside the shark's stomach in no time! Washing the fish with alcohol removed its poison. So did cooking it. After it was cooked it was safe to eat.

What was this powerful poison? The little Moses sole didn't look very special. It looked like any flounder you might see in the supermarket.

Eugenie read that its milk had first been reported in 1871, more than a hundred years before. But nobody knew it was poisonous until Eugenie's discovery.

The Moses sole certainly kept sharks away in the lab's tanks. Now what would happen with big sharks in the sea?

Eugenie and her assistants set out shark lines in the sea, far from shore. They baited the line with different kinds of fish, some alive and some dead. All along the line, in between the other fish — but not too close — they hung the Moses sole.

They set the line during the day. Nothing happened in the daylight hours. Then the sun began to set and the sea darkened. Eugenie and her assistants put on scuba gear and slipped into the water to watch.

The sea was calm and as smooth as glass. Suddenly the water rippled over the shark line. One dark shadow drifted up from the deep. Then another. From the dark depths of the sea, sharks were swimming up. Silently, swiftly, they swam to the little fish wriggling on the line.

The sharks ate up all the fish one by one — all but the Moses sole!

Day after day, Eugenie repeated the test. She noticed that the sharks came to the line most often at dusk and again the next morning, before the sun rose. Each time, they avoided the Moses sole!

One evening, Eugenie's student, Avi Barnes, was swimming along the place where the reef drops down like a wall. Avi signaled to Eugenie to press the button on the underwater camera. The camera lights flashed in the dark sea. Inches away from Avi was a large requiem shark — right near his head!

Eugenie could see the shark's eyes gleaming. She felt goose bumps on her arms. But the shark was not interested in Avi. There were more tempting things for it to eat — like the fish on the line.

And once again, Eugenie saw the shark gobble up all the fish on the line — all but the little Moses sole.

Naftali Primor, one of Eugenie's students in Israel, studied the effects of the milk of the Moses sole. The poison from this little fish has proven more effective than any other chemical shark repellent. A thimbleful of the milky poison could keep hungry sharks away for many hours — eighteen hours in one of the tests. It doesn't wash away in the water like other chemicals.

A suntan lotion company called Eugenie about the Moses sole chemical. They wanted to make a product that prevented sunburn *and* shark attack. But they couldn't make it strong enough to repel the very large sharks, so the lotion was never put on the market.

BOOK TWO

More Adventures of the Shark Lady

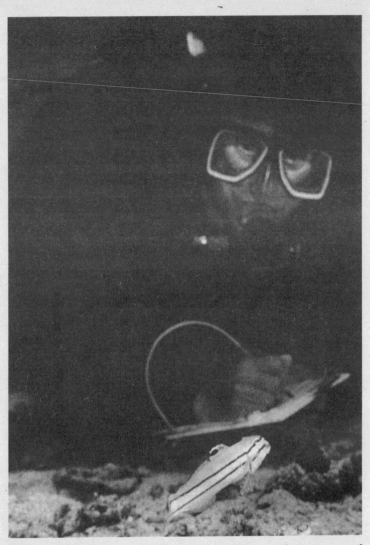

Eugenie Clark writes underwater with a special pen and pad.

13
Diving with Great White Sharks

The great white shark rushed straight toward Eugenie, its mouth wide open. The shark's mighty jaws crunched down on the steel bars a few inches from Eugenie's face. She pressed against the far side of the steel shark cage only to feel another great white shark's nose poking through the cage at her back.

It was 1979 and Dr. Eugenie Clark had come to Dangerous Reef in South Australia to study the great white shark up close. Of all the different kinds of sharks, the great white is the one that strikes the most fear in people's hearts.

Eugenie was with photographer David Doubilet and his wife, Anne. Rodney Fox, an Australian diver, had made all the arrangements. He rented the boat and equipped it with steel cages that were designed to hold divers underwater and protect them from the sharks.

Anne, David, and Eugenie examined the cages closely.

"You may think they look frail," Rodney Fox said, "but they do the job. We haven't lost anybody" — he grinned — "yet!"

Eugenie had made hundreds of dives with different kinds of sharks around the world. But the great white shark was different.

"It's the only shark whose diet is made up of objects as large as humans," she said.

"Did you say humans?" David said. "Hey, that's what we are."

"The great white shark has rarely — if ever — eaten an entire human being," Eugenie said. "It uses the bite-and-spit-out method. Of course, if the bite is big enough, you could lose an arm or a leg, or enough blood to die.

But the great white sharks prefer a meal of other fish, octopuses, and sea lions."

Eugenie knew what kept great whites around Dangerous Reef. There was a colony of sea lions, a favorite meal for the big sharks. Rodney also threw huge amounts of chum — a mixture of blood, meat, and tuna — into the water to bring in the great whites.

Underwater, Eugenie and David were in two separate cages side by side, only ten feet apart. Eugenie had brought her own camera. The great white sharks charged and pounded at the two cages. The cages shook! Steel met steel as sharks more than fourteen feet long kept charging at them. One minute the cages clanged together. The next minute, a shark charged between them and the cages were knocked apart.

Eugenie and David caught glimpses of each other's wide-eyed expressions through their face masks as the sharks crashed against the cages. At one time, they were in the water with five great white sharks swimming around them!

The charging and thrusting were only a small part of the sharks' reaction to the strange human invaders. Most of the time they swam past the cages, so streamlined, so graceful that Eugenie was awestruck by their beauty.

Then suddenly all the sharks disappeared. In the strange silence, Eugenie kept turning slowly around in her cage, wondering from which direction the next shark would come. In a way, this was the spookiest part of the adventure.

It wasn't long before a shark came. Instead of backing against the far side of the cage, she aimed her camera in its face when it swam head-on. Sometimes she even reached through the bars and managed to stroke one as it passed.

Eugenie spent ten days at Dangerous Reef with David, Anne, and Rodney. From the underwater cages, David shot picture after picture of the great white sharks. Eugenie made notes about their behavior. To lure the sharks,

Rodney kept dumping the blood and ground-up tuna bait into the sea. For good measure, he hung chunks of meat under the boat. Often, when Eugenie was in her shark cage, Rodney would pour another messy load overboard and Eugenie would get a shampoo of blood and guts!

Eugenie remembered that, years ago, the great underwater explorer William Beebe called sharks "chinless cowards." Beebe knew, as most experienced scuba divers know, that sharks are usually frightened away by people. But not the great white. Eugenie says, "No amount of commotion, of people taking pictures or whooping and yelling seems to affect it. When it's lured to the boat by the chum, it's the only shark that actually comes to the surface, sticks its head out, and seems to look the boat over."

On the last night, Eugenie and her friends were enjoying a late supper when they heard a heavy thump at the back of the boat. A massive great white was ramming the boat as it stole a fifty-pound bag of tuna bait hanging on the platform, well above the water.

The shark thumped the boat all night, slapping it with its tail and actually lifting the thirty-two-foot boat from below.

14
A Coral Reef in Trouble!

Eugenie Clark floated down in the water. She was in Egypt, at her favorite reef, Ras Mohammed. It was her first scuba dive of the summer of 1980. She couldn't wait to greet her favorite fish friends and the beautiful coral of the Red Sea. Soon she was fifty feet deep.

Here were the masked puffer fish, the parrot fish, and the long-nosed banded pipefish. Here were the lionfish, their fins tipped with poison. She dove through forests of big pink sea fans and swam past colorful corals that looked like they belonged in a fairy tale. A streamlined silvertip shark swam by. The tiny clownfish made her laugh.

Except for the fish, what she saw on the reef that day did not make her laugh. She almost wept at the sight of junk and garbage covering the reef: anchors, ropes, tin cans, bottles, and hundreds of yards of nylon fishing lines and hooks.

Eugenie and her diving friends decided to have an underwater cleanup day. They took bags and bags of junk out of the sea. But the cleanup was only a drop in the bucket. Eugenie knew that something more had to be done to save the reefs.

In the years since she had been coming to Ras Mohammed, the area had become one of the most popular dive sites in the world. Thousands of scuba divers, campers, fishermen, scientists, vacationers, and photographers drove down new roads to get to the beautiful reefs. Boats took divers out. Then an airport was built nearby and people flew in from around the world.

Vacationers dumped their trash into the sea.

Heavy debris tumbled down the steep reef walls. Garbage spread over the once-clean shores. Ras Mohammed was in danger of becoming an underwater dump, a watery wasteland.

And that wasn't all. Fishermen changed from cotton to the stronger nylon fishing lines. The lines and hooks caught on living coral. As the fishermen pulled up the lines, big chunks of coral were broken up. Some fishermen even used dynamite to blast the reefs to kill fish. They dropped their boat anchors, which smashed into the coral reefs. In a few seconds, living coral formations were broken apart — some that scientists say take up to two thousand years to form.

Thousands of years to grow, Eugenie thought. *And only seconds to die.*

Eugenie knew that something had to be done. But what? In 1980, Eugenie met a young Egyptian diver, Gamal Sadat. He introduced Eugenie to his father. Gamal's father was Anwar Sadat, the president of Egypt. Eugenie lost no time in telling President Sadat about the marvels of Ras Mohammed. Then she told him about the threat to the coral reefs. To her great surprise, he said, "I will make Ras Mohammed a national park. That way it can be protected forever."

President Sadat was true to his word. Preparations for the national park were started immediately.

But by the end of the year, everything changed. In 1981, Anwar Sadat was killed by an assassin's bullet! Ras Mohammed Marine Park was forgotten.

Eugenie did not give up. She got her diving friends to write to the new president of Egypt. Conservation groups around the world joined in to save Ras Mohammed.

Their efforts paid off. In 1983, Ras Mohammed became Egypt's first national park.

15
Gentle Giants

In 1983, Eugenie was invited to Mexico. There she would dive with whale sharks, the biggest fish in the sea, in the Sea of Cortez.

The wind was blowing like a gale when she arrived. Eugenie and her friends wondered if they'd ever be able to get in the water with a whale shark. For six days, they waited in safe harbor for the winds to die down. They talked and dreamed of whale sharks, the gentle giants of the sea.

At last the weather changed. Now the pilot could take the spotter plane up to see if there were whale sharks in the area. Soon he radioed to Eugenie and her friends in their boat: "Whale shark right in front of you!" Quickly, the divers put on their scuba gear and plunged into the path of the shark.

It looks like a spaceship! Eugenie thought as she got closer to the harmless monster. Dozens of small remoras were clinging to the whale shark, under its chin and inside its mouth and gill slits.

One of the filmmakers moved in front of the shark, and Eugenie could see just how huge it truly was. The six-foot-tall man looked like a tiny doll next to the shark.

The whale shark paid no attention to the divers. It didn't try to swim away. But even so, Eugenie had to struggle to catch up. Almost out of breath, she reached out and felt its hard, thick skin. Then she grabbed the whale shark's big back dorsal fin and held on to it as the shark continued its downward plunge.

Down, down it went — twenty-five feet . . . thirty feet . . . a hundred feet.

With Eugenie still hanging on, the great shark tilted its head and slid into the depths as

Riding a whale shark was one of the most thrilling adventures of Eugenie's life.

if to say, "Let me take you where no human has ever gone."

Deeper it went and deeper still. Eugenie began to feel sleepy and confused — the dangerous effect of nitrogen narcosis, a condition that happens to divers at extreme depths. At 185 feet, she had to let go.

Back on the surface, Eugenie and her friends were bubbling with excitement. "If I were a remora," Eugenie said, "I would love to ride on that whale shark forever!"

16
Shark Lady in the Grip of a Monster Crab

Eugenie and the photographer David Doubilet were working together on a story for *National Geographic*. They were diving in the waters of Izu Oceanic Park in Japan, home of the giant spider crab.

David needed a good picture of the crab for their story. He was thrilled to find a big one on the sand, 140 feet below the surface. No one had ever photographed the giant crab so deep in the ocean.

David gave Eugenie an underwater signal. Eugenie understood that he wanted her to come closer and lift the crab's head so that he could get a great photo. The only way Eugenie could lift the crab's huge head was to get behind it and reach over its back. So, scuba tank and all, she crept up behind the crab, dug her flippers into the sand, and pulled up on the crab's head.

But the crab didn't want its head pulled up. It tried to break Eugenie's hold, but it needed to brace itself against something — and the only thing close enough was Eugenie's leg! Before she knew it, the crab had wrapped one of its legs around her thigh, and another around her other leg.

This was no ordinary crab that was holding Eugenie prisoner below the sea. It was a member of the largest crab species in the world. From the tip of one outstretched claw to the other, these crabs grow to twelve feet across, the size of two tall men lying end to end. Its eyes, on stalks, move independently and look forward, backward, and sideways.

Trapped by a giant crab! Eugenie thought of

what the Japanese call this monster — *shinin gani* — dead man's crab. It is known to feed on the bodies of people who drown in the sea.

Quickly she put that thought out of her mind and concentrated on getting free. Each time she pulled the crab's head up a little, the crab pulled down as if they were playing a game of strength. She managed to unlock one of the crab's legs from her thigh. Still holding on to its head, she struggled to get her other leg free.

Divers were holding big lights so that David

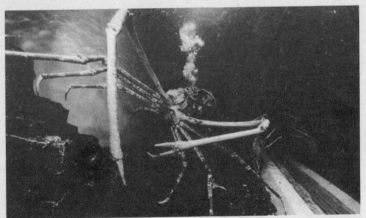

© David Doubilet

Eugenie grabs the head of the giant spider crab. The crab's head is almost as large as hers!

could get his picture. Eugenie felt like she and the crab were the stars of some weird movie. She laughed to herself as she thought of the movie's title: *Shark Lady in the Grip of a Monster Crab!*

The divers had only a few more minutes before they had to start up to the surface. They were in danger of getting "the bends," the dreaded disease that scuba divers can get when they dive too deep for too long. The bends can cripple, or even kill, a person.

The crab started to walk sideways, carrying Eugenie away from the lights and camera.

The crab was heading straight for some rocks! But it didn't bash Eugenie against them. Now it could hold on to the rocks, not Eugenie's legs, to push against her. Eugenie had to let go. David got some good pictures, and Eugenie got another underwater adventure she would never forget.

17
Down to Two
Thousand Feet

Down, down, the submersible sank with Eugenie Clark inside. She was off the coast of Bermuda in the Atlantic Ocean in her first dive in a submersible craft.

Eugenie peered through the plastic window, fascinated by the strange underwater world. Thousands of tiny creatures, the size of sugar crystals, formed a cloud of reddish sparks. Worms flashed through the cloud like shooting stars. A silvery blue fish, only three inches long, shot into view. It stood on its head and began to bounce like a pogo stick.

Eugenie checked her watch. She could

hardly believe half an hour had passed so fast. Just a little while ago, she was at sea level, safely aboard the fishing boat *Miss Wendy*.

Now she was cramped in the small sub called *Pisces VI* with the pilot and Emory Kristof of the National Geographic Society. Emory was too tall to stand up straight in the six-foot sphere. Much of the space was taken up with instruments.

In only a few minutes, I've already gone deeper than I've ever been using scuba, Eugenie realized.

The pilot's radio announcement interrupted her excited thoughts.

"*Pisces VI* to *Miss Wendy*. We are at one thousand feet. One, zero, zero, zero."

Light flashed in the inky waters. Emory was grinning. His video cameras were working fine, lighting up a saber-toothed viper fish with fangs as long as its head. And a silvery hatchet fish was gleaming like tinsel.

Like Alice in an underwater wonderland, Eugenie peered through the "looking glass" of *Pisces VI*.

"*Pisces VI* to *Miss Wendy*. We are passing thirteen hundred feet. One, three, zero, zero," was the next radio announcement from the pilot.

Eugenie began to feel cold and clammy.

Oh, no, she thought. She looked at the walls of the sub and saw droplets of water. *Could the submersible be leaking?* She turned to the pilot who didn't look at all worried.

"The water's cold this deep down," he said. "The warm air in here and our breath is turning into water and it's dripping down the cold walls."

Eugenie took out a warm jacket from the bag she had brought on board. Inside the bag were three chocolate bars, a cheese sandwich, and a plastic mayonnaise jar. There was no room for a bathroom in the sub. That was what the mayonnaise jar was for. She also had a notebook and pen to write down everything she saw.

The pilot spotted a good place to set the submersible down. For a moment the sub hovered like a spacecraft about to land on the moon. Then it settled down on the bottom.

The pilot spoke again into the radio: "*Pisces VI* to *Miss Wendy*. We have landed at two thousand feet. Two, zero, zero, zero."

The pilot turned off the lights inside the sub. "We're really at the bottom of the sea!"

It was lucky that Eugenie was not a worrier. She knew about the possible dangers. The batteries of the submersible could run out. Or the sub could spring a leak that would mean instant death. But she trusted the *Pisces VI*. It had made hundreds of dives safely.

Looking through the window at the night world outside, Eugenie could see a dim green glow. This came from chemical sticks that were tied to a cage attached to a mechanical arm coming out from the sub. The cage was baited with tuna.

The divers waited for the sharks to come.

Eugenie had studied shallow-water sharks all over the world. Now she might see the deep-sea sharks: the giant six-gill, the rare megamouth, or the goblin shark, which no one had ever seen alive.

A large eye with a fish's body loomed in the distance. It was too far away for Eugenie to tell what it was. The eye shone like a cat's eye, reflecting the dim light.

Suddenly she heard a noise, like teeth chomping on metal. The sub rocked and lifted slightly. Then a huge head came from underneath the sub, and the green eye of a shark was looking in. Eugenie thought it was looking right at her!

This was a six-gill shark. "It must be eighteen feet long!" Emory said. "As big as a truck."

As the shark battered the submersible, Eugenie had her first up-close look at the speckled six-gill. It had parasites hanging from its fins, like babies riding a magic carpet.

She wrote pages of notes, describing every detail of the new creatures. "The sharks move as in a dream or a slow-motion movie," she wrote.

She drew pictures of the strange world two

thousand feet deep. The tapioca fish, never before seen alive, "looks like a huge, chocolate barracuda," she wrote. It had big teeth and a hook on each scale.

Four hours had gone by. It was time to go up. Eugenie had completely lost track of time in the eerie blackness.

Before they reached the surface, Emory was planning the next submersible dive. What other marvels lay waiting for them in the depths of the sea?

Eugenie aboard the Pisces, *one of many submersibles that took her down into the deep sea.*

18
More Deep-Sea Dives

Back on *Miss Wendy*, Eugenie and Emory congratulated each other. Emory had gotten first-ever photos and movies of giant sharks in the deep sea. And for Eugenie, another one of her dreams had come true. She had seen some of the creatures that her longtime hero, scientist William Beebe, had written about long ago.

Back in 1934, Beebe went half a mile beneath the sea in an underwater craft called a *bathysphere*. He told about a fantastic new world and creatures with huge fangs and hinged mouths. He wrote about them in books and magazine articles that Eugenie read when she was eleven years old. Eugenie dreamed of someday exploring these hidden depths, of seeing what Beebe saw.

Now, more than fifty years later, she had actually seen the hatchet fish, the viper fish, and the deep-sea eels he had described. And she had seen fishes that Dr. Beebe had never seen — like the sharks.

The fishing boat, *Miss Wendy*, belonged to Eugenie's friend Teddy Tucker, a shipwreck explorer and deep-sea fisherman who lived in Bermuda. Teddy got the idea of attaching green glowing chemical sticks to his fishing lines. Fish were attracted by the glowing lights. The lights looked like *photophores*, the glowing organs of deep-sea fish that lure their prey.

Teddy and another local fisherman, called Blue-Eye Billy, knew about the deep places in the sea where the rare four-eyed sharks swam. And where there were many big six-gill sharks. But no one had actually seen the big sharks swimming in the deep sea before. When submersibles go down to repair oil lines, they carry lights but no bait. Their bright underwater lights shine only on an empty sea bottom.

William Beebe hadn't seen any deep-sea sharks, either, when he went half a mile down in 1934. He wasn't able to land on the bottom where the sharks dwell. He was afraid the cable holding his bathysphere might tangle in cliffs or debris. He called the bathysphere "a pea in the sea, hanging by a spidery thread." He never carried a bait cage.

It was Emory's idea to use a submersible as a blind, or hiding place. He wanted to carry fish bait in cages to bring in the creatures of the deep and photograph them.

With Teddy Tucker's help, Emory started the Beebe Project, named after Eugenie's childhood hero. Eugenie joined the Beebe Project as chief scientist.

It took more than a year of planning, designing, and testing. Emory attached cameras to the sub. The bait cage was loaded with chunks of dead fish and bloody fish guts. Teddy's green glowing chemical sticks were tied to the

Emory Kristoff went with Eugenie on many submersible dives.

bait cage, and the cage was carried down by the mechanical arm on the submersible.

Then the pilot turned off the inside light and backed the sub away from the cage. After a while, the sharks came in, attracted by the lights and the fishy smell of the bait.

Eugenie and Emory saw tapioca fish in the deep sea. And they saw all kinds of sharks: the biggest living six-gill sharks, glowing lantern sharks, bigfin gummy sharks, cat sharks, cigar sharks, and gulper sharks.

Eugenie was busy making notes and drawing pictures in her notebooks about all the fascinating fish that came into view that day. She was making important scientific discoveries.

In later dives off the coasts of Bermuda, Japan, and California, Eugenie went down even deeper. Once, off Bermuda, she went down 3,800 feet. She saw huge creatures, like the fifteen-foot elephant ear sponge, the largest sponge ever seen. She saw small creatures, such as the sea dandelion, looking like a tiny burst of fireworks. She saw weird sea gulpers that look like snakes with huge heads and hinged mouths that open like a garbage truck to swallow their prey.

Eugenie filled notebook after notebook with descriptions of these and other oddities of the deep sea: large, bright-red deep-water shrimps, with enormous long antennae like a weird bunch of carrots; anglerfish that sometimes attack prey that is larger than themselves; and snub-nosed eels that burrow into the body of their prey, eating it from the inside out.

Eugenie's notebooks are filled with pages like this, with detailed drawings and important data.

Once she saw a red blob, as startling as a splash of blood. As the sub came closer, Eugenie saw the blob lift slightly and shoot into the open water. Eugenie saw that the blob was actually a squid more than a foot long.

One of Eugenie's biggest surprises was the twenty-inch cigar-shaped green-eyed cookie-cutter shark. At night it swims up to the surface to attack large fish, and even dolphins and whales. The cookie-cutter gets its teeth tightly into its victim. When its prey tries to get away, the shark hangs on and twists its body around in a circle. It pulls a cookie — a plug of skin and flesh — out of the body of its victim.

From 1987 to 1990, Eugenie was in charge of seventy-one submersible dives. She made fifty-one of the dives herself. Her deepest dive was in the U.S. submersible *Alvin*, to twelve thousand feet — more than two miles down! Her longest dive was seventeen and half hours, in the Russian submersible *Mir*, which means "peace."

19
Whale Sharks
of Ningaloo Reef

It was March 1991. Eugenie was in Australia working on a new story for *National Geographic* magazine about one of her favorite subjects — the giant whale shark. She had never forgotten the wonderful whale shark ride she took eight years before in Mexico.

She wanted to learn more about this gentle giant, so she had come to Ningaloo Reef, Australia's biggest marine park. All fish in the park, including the whale shark, are protected from hunters. Once again, as in Mexico, David Doubilet came along to take pictures for Eugenie's article.

Eugenie and David, dressed in scuba gear, had gone down into the deep waters of the reef. Now a whale shark, all thirty feet and ten tons of it, was swimming toward them. David moved in front of the giant fish to photograph its enormous mouth as it was feeding. He was not afraid. He knew that whale sharks don't eat large animals like people. They feed on small fish and plankton, mainly the tiny shrimplike krill.

By the end of the day, Eugenie and David counted twenty whale sharks. They were overjoyed. Many marine scientists have never even seen one.

Eugenie was at Ningaloo Reef at the right time. The conditions were ideal for whale sharks because the food supply was at its best.

About a week after the March full moon is when corals spawn. Corals contain thousands and thousands of living animals called *polyps*. Then dense schools of small fish are attracted to this "plankton soup." After spawning, it's not long before whales, manta rays, and whale sharks arrive to feed.

Eugenie had never before dived during a coral spawning. "It's like being at a party celebration where everyone releases miniature pink and white balloons," she said to David.

Eugenie was fascinated by the whale sharks' feeding behavior. The animal swims slowly through a dense ball of plankton on the surface of the water, moving its head from side to side, sucking in the food like a vacuum cleaner.

At Ningaloo Reef, David warned Eugenie about diving too deep. "Remember," he said, "we've got lots of whale sharks around. Stay near the surface so I can get the best light for pictures. Don't go below fifty feet! Check your depth gauge!"

Eugenie caught on to the dorsal fin of a young twenty-foot whale shark. The clean design of its white spots reminded Eugenie of a set of dark blue-and-white dominoes. David was looking through the viewfinder of his camera, taking close-up portraits of the shark's head.

Eugenie and the shark swam down even

deeper. Eugenie felt she was being towed through the water by a living submarine. Then she checked her depth gauge. She and David were already below a hundred feet! That was twice as deep as they meant to go. Eugenie let go of the shark and they headed for the surface.

In their dives that month, the two divers began to recognize individual whale sharks by their scars, line patterns, and spots. They saw two hundred whale sharks in all — more than Eugenie dreamed possible.

Eugenie went back to Ningaloo Reef the next year. There was a new rule then — no more riding on whale sharks. A lot of visitors wanted to ride the sharks, and the people in charge were worried that the sharks were being disturbed. In a way, Eugenie was disappointed, but she saw that the new rule was needed for the protection of the gentle giants she so admired.

20
Eugenie Makes a Movie

Eugenie was used to being in front of cameras. By 1992, she had appeared in twenty-four television shows. But this IMAX movie, *The Search for the Great Sharks*, was different. The special IMAX cameras and their huge forty-foot screens (the height of a four-story building) make moviegoers feel they are underwater.

The filming of *The Search for the Great Sharks* began in 1991. Eugenie flew to Dangerous Reef in Australia, where she had studied great white sharks. One of her students at the University of Maryland, Karen Moody, was invited, too. Karen had never seen a live shark except in the aquarium. She had dissected dead sharks with Eugenie in the lab. Now she'd be diving with the most dreaded sharks in the world — the great whites.

The IMAX moviemakers used "movie magic" tricks for the shark cage. Instead of steel, their cages were made out of clear transparent plastic. The clear plastic made it look as if the divers were in the open seas with the great white sharks — as though the shark cages weren't there at all!

Eugenie and Karen were together in one cage. Suddenly, a great white rushed toward them and bumped the front of the cage — hard. Eugenie glanced at Karen to see how she was taking her first encounter. But Karen was nowhere to be seen. Where was she? There was no way she could have left the cage. The trapdoor on top wasn't open.

Eugenie looked to the right and to the left. Then she looked down. There was Karen, on

A special plastic shark "cage" was used in the IMAX movie.

her hands and knees between Eugenie's legs. The shark had scared her! After a while, though, Karen got used to having great whites swimming around her, just like Eugenie.

Diving with great white sharks was tame compared with what happened later. They were filming more scenes for the movie off Catalina Island, in California. Eugenie and shark expert Rodney Fox were diving with blue sharks, another dangerous group. The movie people wanted Eugenie to put on a chain-mail suit, like medieval armor, for protection. But Eugenie knew how to act around sharks. She didn't want to wear the heavy suit.

Rodney put on the suit at the director's request. The scene was set. Eugenie would come down from one direction, Rodney from another. They were supposed to meet at the baited cage where dozens of blue sharks would surround them.

There was a current running in the sea, so they planned to make a "drift dive." In a drift dive, the photographers, the cage with the bait to attract the sharks, and the boat above would drift along with the current.

Eugenie and Rodney dove thirty feet below and drifted along, too. The waters beneath them plunged down to three thousand feet. They both wore Scubafone helmets, which served as both face mask and phone, so that they could talk and listen to each other.

The director signaled "Action." As they had planned, Eugenie swam to the bait cage. But there was no sign of Rodney. Then Eugenie heard his chilling words on the Scubafone: "Help, I'm in trouble!"

"Where are you?" Eugenie asked. "Rodney, what's the matter?"

There was no answer. Eugenie spoke urgently to the people on the boat. "Rodney's not here. I don't see him anywhere in the water. There's only one direction he could have gone. Down."

Down meant three thousand feet. And three thousand feet meant death.

Rodney's wife, Kay, was waiting on the boat.

Eugenie could imagine how terrified Kay was feeling. Over and over again, the captain called Rodney on the Scubafone. There was no reply.

At last the captain of the boat shouted, "There he is!" He pointed to a figure far from the boat.

Rodney was hauled out of the water, alive but exhausted. He was no longer wearing his Scubafone.

He gasped out his story. "I was swimming along when one of my flippers came off. I saw the flipper begin to sink. Without thinking, I dove down to get it. I should have known better. My dive suit compressed. Then the chain-mail suit acted like an anchor. Down I went. The deeper I went, the faster I dropped. I reached for my inflator hose, which would bring me back to the surface, but it was caught in all the extra gear I was wearing."

Everyone fell silent, thinking how close Rodney had come to dying. He went on with his story. "With my last bit of reason, I began to take off my equipment. When I pulled off the helmet, I found my inflator hose and I could inflate air into my vest. I came up, probably too fast."

Without his helmet, Rodney couldn't breathe in, but he let out the pressurized air from his lungs as he rose and prevented worse problems.

Rodney was rushed to the hospital. Eugenie thought it was a miracle that he was okay.

"You couldn't get me into one of those suits," Eugenie said later. "Rodney's experience was an example of danger from human error and equipment, not from sharks."

Rodney got well, and the filming went on. In one scene, a blue shark is biting Rodney's arm. To make the shark come to him, Rodney first pulled a dead fish over his arm.

"The director wanted a dramatic scene, but you really have to coax the shark to bite you," Eugenie said when she was asked about the movie. "And the IMAX cameras make the sharks look much bigger than they actually were. Blue sharks get to be longer than ten feet, but most of the ones we saw were smaller, six to eight feet. They look huge in the movie."

The movie was shown in IMAX theaters everywhere and later came out in videocassette and DVD versions. It made Eugenie even more famous than ever. Now millions of people knew about the remarkable Shark Lady and the remarkable discoveries she had made.

Afterword

Eugenie Clark's hair is gray now. She's a grandmother to a teenager. But what a grandmother! She still travels to remote places around the world, studying sharks or fish that no one has studied before.

These days she dives down deep under the sea, halfway around the world, to observe the behavior of small, rare fish. The fish she is studying now is called the convict blenny because of the striped markings on its body. Its scientific name is *Pholidichthys leucotaenia*. Eugenie and her team find these rare fish in deep tunnels in coral reefs. They discovered swarms of two thousand young convict blennies feeding on plankton during the day, and then returning to their parents at dusk. The young fish stay with their parents all night in a tunnel system. They hang by their heads from the ceilings of the tunnels by threads of slimy mucous. Then, at dawn, they leave the tunnels to feed. Eugenie and her team were the first in the world to see and photograph this amazing fish behavior.

She is hard at work at Mote Marine Laboratory in Sarasota, Florida, near her home overlooking the water. At the lab, she has built glass-sided artificial tunnels where she studies the juvenile convict blennies and observes their behavior as they grow to adulthood.

Eugenie was director of Mote Marine Lab way back in 1955, when it was called Cape Haze. Now she has fancy titles — Trustee Emerita and Eminent Scientist — but everybody at Mote knows her as the hardworking Shark Lady, busy at the lab, or in her second-floor office writing her handwritten notes into journals.

Eugenie will never lose her interest in learning about sharks and other creatures of the sea.

In 1996, Eugenie married her old friend, Yoppe. He died in 2000. She looks back to the days when they shared happy times on ocean cruises and he taught her to love playing bridge. Yoppe was with her on a special expedition to the South Pacific the first time Eugenie and her team caught an adult convict blenny.

Eugenie's daughter, Hera, has followed in her mother's footsteps, studying ichthyology and specializing in sharks. She has even named a new species of deep-sea shark. Hera's husband, Coz Cozzi, a doctor, is a nautical archeologist. Eugenie's younger daughter, Aya, is a commercial airline captain. She was one of the first women to become a jet pilot. Both of Eugenie's sons, Tak and Niki, are prize-winning photographers as well as avid pianists. Tak also works for a real estate company in Florida, and Nikki is an underwater stage manager for Cirque du Soleil in Las Vegas.

Mote Marine Laboratory has a new research ship — the *RV Eugenie Clark*. Her grandson, Eli, put on safety goggles when he and Eugenie christened it, smashing a bottle of champagne against the ship's bow. Eli has been on several diving expeditions with his grandmother. His main hobby is BMX bicycle racing, and he wins many trophies. He has the honor of representing Florida in competitions.

People often ask Eugenie if she has ever been attacked by a shark. "Only once," is her answer. Once the teeth of a twelve-foot tiger shark sank into her arm and made it bleed. But the accident didn't happen in the water! She was driving to a school to talk to children about sharks. Beside her, on the front seat, was the dried and mounted jaw of a tiger shark. The traffic light turned from green to red. She slammed on the brakes. At the same time, she stretched out her arm to keep the mounted jaw from falling off the seat, and the jaw fell against her arm!

That was the only time a shark's tooth ever bit the Shark Lady.

Ann McGovern

New York, NY
2004

Index